From Ashes to Angel Light

Rebecca's Pathways Vol. 2

Rebecca J. Steiger

ISBN 978-1-964462-97-4 (Paperback)
ISBN 978-1-964462-98-1 (Ebook)

Inquiries and Book Orders should be addressed to:

Leavitt Peak Press
17901 Pioneer Blvd Ste L #298, Artesia, California 90701
Phone #: 2092191548

Contents

Dedication

I want to thank all those who helped bring me to a higher consciousness. For understanding that all may not be as it seems. For your trust and faith in me and my gift of healing others with word.

Especially my Children Amy and Andy.

In 1993, I was in a horrendous experience! The Tornado that blew my four-year-old grandson clinging to my chest, out of a house. We landed out in a field away from where the house use to be. We were surrounded by downed live electrical lines in the pouring rain, the dark and never even knew they were there. We got up and walked off without a scratch. I was hit in the head by something, and the next thing I know I was standing in a shaft of light, I was no larger than a head of a straight pen, and I was standing before God and His Supreme presence! What I felt was peace in a loving presence. He told me I had many things to do. He sent us back to do deliver His message to you! I write this book for other, so that you too can stand in the Light of Ever Lasting Love. That heals us all. The most horrendous thing that happened to me ended up being the biggest gift I have ever received from this life. My Blessing.

When Spirit knocks on your door make sure you are listening! Look for the signs, learn the lessons and receive the gifts.

"Stand in your own light of higher consciousness."

Preface

I want to thank everyone who helped lead me a very ordinary person, from my own darkness, in the Light of everlasting love. My friends who stood by me, my family, and especially to my clients and readers of my books. They are the true believers in my work.

Introduction

This book is a self-help book. Opening your mind to an Angelic realm of possibilities. HOW SCARY! To leave your safe little world of darkness, entering a world of conscious thought. Standing in the light of peace and Love. Leaving all those behind, that cannot see and are afraid to truly live. Those who huddle in darkness of the mind.

Change is the thing you fear most. Being different or seeming odd to others. Your family, friends, your co-hearts. Let me tell you this. Change can be the most exciting, rewarding thing you may ever do. Bing able to think outside the box. Being able to truly see and be who you always dreamed of being, making it a reality. Through change and light healing of the mind, you will shine, you will prosper. You will enter a new an wonderful world of understanding.

I wrote this book for you. For you alone.

By helping yourself, you will help others. By healing yourself, you will heal those around you. How? By being a bacon of light, by letting go of your stress and worries, others will start relaxing and feeling the warmth that radiates within and around you. They to will start to feel. You do not know whom it might help heal.

So, if you open your mind and choose to accept change. Choose the path of light and healing. Awareness of the mind awaits you. Enjoy the journey. What a wonderful life awaits you. Go forth and drink in the light, like the finest wine.

Discover the channels that will open for you. Do not fear them, for they are a gift from Spirit! Use them to benefit of others, as well as yourself. Doors will open; all you must do is walk through them. Life is so simple, once you accept change in a positive way. Finding peace and joy on this Heavenly earth. Letting go of fear and stress is the hard part., having trust in what you do and who you are. Why?

Because you have worn fear and stress like a second skin. You have been programmed to feel stress ad worry, to be like everyone else. When you were a small child, someone said to you be careful, you could fall. You could fail. If you never fall, then how can you truly know when you're upright? If you never fail, how can you feel the joy of success?

Life is a journey of wonders and miracles. Learning and receiving gifts. Giving and receiving from one another. Join me on this roller coaster ride called life. Feel the thrill of rising high and the heart in your throat, going faster, up and down than you ever thought possible. Flying higher, with one foot on the ground. Spinning your head as if you are dancing a waltz.

Feel the freedom to laugh, cry, dance with joy or sing with the Heavenly voices of the birds.

The adventure is great, won't you come along and enjoy living life to the fullest. Breathing, loving and surrounding you with peace and light. Having trust in all things. The choice of course, is yours.

Do not ask if this is what you are to do. Just listen to your heart and your inner self. No one knows you better than you do! You know your heart beast, you know your secret thoughts, and you know your feelings better than anyone, except God! For he hears your heartbeat, your thoughts, your feelings. He is the only Supreme Being who knows you better than you do. So quiet your mind and let Spirit shows you the way. Be specific in your choices, be firm in your beliefs. What is your intent? What is your choice?

What we need are eyes to see and ears to hear. Use what God has given you. See what you see, look at the whole of things and not just a tiny fragment. Hear beyond the word and now. Listen to those who speak, especially your inner self. Know and put out there what you want in life. Be positive. Be sure of yourself and make your own decisions, most of all do not have doubt, do not fear your intent. Be positive in what you believe. What is right for you, meant for you, may not be the same as someone else. That is why we are called individuals. That is why everyone needs something different from the next person. Find out who you are. Make that self-discovery.

All of us enjoy special taste. A great dinner. We all get that special, warm feeling when we taste or buy something great! Wouldn't you like to keep that feeling of contentment all the time? Of course, we are not fools. Well, when you open yourself to living and loving, changing and evolving, you will have that special warmth and comfort with you always. It cost you nothing and it will fill you up: no hidden hunger. Just warmth, peace and sincerity. Joy!

When I first began my journey, I too wondered what others would think? Blocking all I could out. However, God will not let you look back; He will not let you worry. For when you learn, as I did, to let Spirit and the Angelic realm handle things, then all becomes as it should be. People will accept, understand, and look to you for guidance. So, all it takes is faith and trust in yourself. Faith in the higher power of life. It does not matter if you call God, or Buddha, whoever. Know that I have stood before the higher power, God or Spirit, Mother, Father or Child. I know the wisdom, strength and love given freely to us all. Live in the moment, because that is what you have now! This moment. There is no tomorrow until today, this moment is done.

Reap the rewards of living in a life full of choices, love peace and intention.

How would you feel if you had no fear of being alone? Of death? Of going somewhere alone, without someone else to guide you, to protect you? When you are aligned with Spirit, the Angelic realm you will realize that strength, protection, and love is always around and everlasting. That you are never alone and that all is as it should be.

You will become secure in your decisions; and you will no longer fear death or loneliness. You will start to really breath, live and love life on this Heavenly earth. It does not matter your age, sex, where you are, who you are with. You have the choice of opening into yourself and finding your God source, your inner strength, your peace and place in your life. Remember, to listen and see. Give and share, then you too will also receive.

We all have to live with man upon this earth. Meet certain obligations. Pay for utilities, rent food and all the things that go along with it. We have to live with man. These things can be done much easier when we open ourselves to abundance! Do not block your monetary flow; you might be surprised where it comes from. Do not give your work or gifts away. Make it worth paying for. If you want abundance, all you have to do is ask for it, and it will be yours. Be confident in yourself and your self-worth. Believe in yourself. Let Spirit and the Angels take care of the hard things, you just enjoy life. Dance with the sun and sing a song of joy. Why not? All is as it should be.

Be the powerful person you were meant to be. Surround yourself with light, letting it shine ahead of you, lighting your way. Will never falter when you are in the light. By lighting your path, you also help and show the way for others. Be aware of all things around you but most of all be aware of yourself though you God self. Though love. Finding strength and conviction to live a positive life. Of course, the choice is yours. Life is a choice, we choose to learn, and from whom, we give, we love, we laugh, and we keep going forward in life. We then receive the gifts!

Life's greatest challenge is letting go of the restrains we have put on ourselves. Letting go of the restrains we have put on ourselves. Letting go of the past and being free. Flying through life to be who you were meant to be. Spirit created you, shaped you and loves you. Let Spirit and the Angels take care of the hard thins, enjoy life. Dance with the sun and sing a song of joy. Why not? All is as it should be.

Be the powerful person you were meant to be. Surround yourself with light, letting it shine ahead of you, lighting your path. You will never falter when you are in the light. By lighting your path, you also help light and show the way for others. Be aware of all things around you, be aware of yourself though your God self. Through Love. Finding strength and conviction to live. Of course, the choice is yours. Life is a choice, we choose to learn, fand from whom, we give, we love, we laugh, and we keep going forward in life. We then receive the gifts! Find yourself in these pages and get ready to start a new and exciting life.

Chapter One

This Is Called the Wrath of God

This is a book for your mind, body, and spirit connection. Opening your mind to an Angelic Realm of possibilities. To Leave your safe little world of darkness and entering a world of conscious thought. Standing in the light of peace and love. Leaving all those behind, that cannot see and are afraid to truly live, those who huddle in darkness of the mind. All things that instill fear. For fear leaches out the energy of life, never letting you move forward in a positive, and loving way. By cutting the cords of fear and negativity, you move to a world of wonderment, to fine the peace and tranquility you are seeking.

Change is the thing you fear most. Being different or seeming odd to others. Your family, friends, your co-hearts let me tell you this; Change can be the most exciting, rewarding thing you may ever do. Being able to think outside of the box. Being able to truly see and be who you always dreamed of being. Making it a reality. Through change and light healing of the mind, you will shine, you will prosper. You will enter a new and wonderful world of understanding. However, making and accepting changes in your life can also be exciting and rewarding. Thinking outside the box will allow yourself to truly see, to make your dream of being who you always wanted to be into a reality. Through change and light healing of the mind, you will shine and prosper. For you become a shining star of light that will help you shine and understand not only yourself, but others better in this life. Letting you know what a powerful being you truly are.

I wrote this book for you alone.

The biggest change that you will experience in life is when the Angels come to take you from this Earth to your heavenly home. Your physical form is left behind and you continue to life in a different form and a different way. You will cross the veil and live between two worlds, Heaven and Earth. Really, there is no difference as Earth is an extension of Heaven.

By helping yourself, you will help others. By healing yourself, you will heal those around you. How? By being a beacon of light and letting go of your stress and worries. Others too will then start to feel the warmth that shines within and around you. How? By letting go of your stress and worries, others will start relaxing and feeling the warmth that radiates within and around you. They too will start to feel, to heal.

By opening your mind and accepting yourself, others will start to accept you as you were truly meant to be. By helping yourself, you will send the breath of life around the world and who knows where it might land. You do not know whom it might help heal.

So, if you open your mind and choose to accept change, choose the path of light and healing. Awareness of the mind awaits you, enjoy the journey. What a wonderful life awaits you. You can have a wonderful life ahead, if you open your mind, body and spirit. Go forth and drink in the light, like the finest wine.

Discover the channels that will open for you. Do not fear them, for they are your gift from Spirit! Use them for the benefit of others, as well as yourself. Doors will open, all you have to do is walk through them. Life is so simple, once you accept change in a positive way. Finding peace and joy on this Heavenly earth. Letting go of stress and fear is the hard part, having trust in in what you do and who you are. Why? Because you have worn fear and stress like a second skin. You have been programmed to feel stress and worry, to be like everyone else. When you were a small child, someone said to you, be careful you could fall! You could fail. If you never fall, then how can you truly know when your upright? If you never fail, how can you feel the joy of success? Accepting change in a positive way, can then lead you to find that life is so simple, and you will feel peace and joy on this heavenly Earth.

Life is a journey of wonders and miracles. lessons and gifts, giving and receiving from one another. Join me on this roller coaster ride called life. Feel the thrill of rising high, with your heart in your throat, climbing higher and going faster than you ever thought possible. Flying higher, with one foot on the ground. Spinning your head as if you are dancing a waltz.

Feel the freedom to laugh and cry, dance with joy or sing with the heavenly voices of the birds. The adventure is great, won't you come along and enjoy living life to the fullest? Breathing, loving and surrounding you with peace and light. Having trust in all things. The Choice of course is yours.

Do not ask if this is what you are to do, just listen to your heart and your inner self. No one knows you better than you do! You know your heartbeat, you know your inner thoughts and you know your feelings better than anyone, except God! He hears your heartbeat, your thoughts and your feelings. He is the only Supreme Being who knows you better than you do. So, quieten your mind and let Spirit show you the way. Be specific in your choices, be firm in your beliefs. What are your choices?

What we need are eyes to see and ears that hear. Use what God has given you. See what you see, look at the whole of things and not just a tiny fragment. Hear beyond the whole of things and not just tiny fragments. Hear beyond the word and the now. Listen to those who speak, especially your inner self. Know and put out there what you want in life. Be positive. Be sure of yourself and make your own decisions, but most of all do not have doubt and do not fear your intent. Be positive in what you believe. What is right for you and meant for you, may not be the same as for someone else. That is why we are called individuals. That is why everyone needs something different from the next person. Find out who you are and make that discovery.

All of us enjoy that special taste, that make us feel, warm inside. A great dinner. A wonderful rich dessert. Wouldn't you like to keep that feeling of contentment all the time? Of course, we would. Well, when you open yourself to living and loving, changing and evolving, you will have that special warmth and comfort with you always. It cost you nothing and it will fill you up. No hidden hunger, just warmth, peace, serenity and joy!

When I first began my journey, I too wondered what others would think. I blocked out everything I could out. However, God will not let you look back. He will not let you worry. When you learn, as I did, to let Spirit and the Angelic Realm handle things, then all becomes as it should be. People will accept, understand and look to you for guidance. All it takes is faith and trust in yourself and in the higher power of life. Live in the moment because that is what you have now… The moment! There is no tomorrow until today is in the past, this moment is done.

Reap the rewards of living in a life full of choices, love, peace and intention. How would you feel if you had no fear of being alone? No fear of death? Going somewhere alone, without someone else to guide and protect you? When you are attuned with Spirit and the Angelic realm, you will realize that strength, protection and love is always around and everlasting. You will never be alone and that all is as it should be. You will become secure in your decisions. You will no longer fear death or loneliness. You will start to breath, live and love life on this heavenly Earth. It does not matter what your gender is, how old you are, where you are or anything else. You have the choice of opening into yourself and finding your God source, your inner strength, your peace and place in your life. Remember, to listen and see. Give and share, then you too will also receive.

We all must live with each other upon this Earth. We must meet certain obligations and pay for necessities such as utilities, rent, food and everything else we need for survival. We must live with man. These things can be done much easier when we open ourselves to abundance! Do not block your monetary flow, as you might be surprised where it comes from. Do not give your work away. Make it worth paying for. If you want abundance, all you have to do is ask for it and it will be yours. Be confident in yourself and your self-worth. Believe in yourself. Let Spirit and the angels take care of the hard things. Enjoy your life, dance with the sun and sing a song of joy. Why not? All is as it should be.

Be the powerful person you were meant to be. Surround yourself with light and let it shine ahead of you, lighting your path. You will never falter when you are in the light, and you will also help light and show the way for others. Be aware of all things around you, be aware of yourself through your god self. Through love you will find the strength and conviction to live. Of course, the choice is yours. Life is a choice; we choose to learn and from whom. We give, we love, we laugh, and we keep going forward in life. We then receive the gifts!

Life's greatest challenge is letting go of the restrains we have put on ourselves. Letting go of the past, being free. Flying through life, to be who you were meant to be. Spirit created you, shaped you and loves you.

Chapter Two

ANGELS AND PATHWAYS

Angels, the messengers! Traveling well-worn paths from heaven to earth in a nanosecond and weaving through our daily lives. Angels bring us comfort, care for us when we are sick, lighten our days and protect us from harm. When you feel a light touch from a loved one that has crossed over, the Angels have led them to you to comfort you in your sorrow.

I know, because I have seen them. They deliver messages, they are omnipresent and stand with us 24 hours a day, 7 days a week. You can refuse to talk to them, and you can even send them away, but they will still be there in your hour of need. They will help you here on Earth and they will show you the way home, when your time in this life is done.

The Universe is busy now, leading so many home and taking care of many here on this heavenly Earth that man is trying so hard to destroy. Man is doing his best to block Spirit and the Angelic realm. He is working to leave you in uncertain darkness and helping the antichrist to take over! However, Spirit and his troop of Angels can lead you to the light of love and healing to overcome the antichrist! He will overcome the acts of man and his stupidity, showing you a brighter day and a better and fuller life.

The days of darkness are here but will be followed by the light days of growing and harvesting of all things on this Earth. A clean sweep will be made, and peace will come over all of us. Anger and hate will be dissolved, and love will prevail to fill the void, making your life a joy and not a chore. Bring joy within you now through the Angels, through Spirit and through the light of day. Let go of the darkness and let man have their sorrow on his lost ship of hope.

By bringing peace for one person, you light them up! You see, it is a chain reaction! If you smile and radiate a happy and positive energy, it becomes infectious. It is a soothing and wonderful gift that you not only give to yourself, but also to others. Living through God and the Angelic realm, you can truly see the rainbow of life. Lighting and balancing the many colors in your life will take away the pain, hurt and anger while replacing it with love, trust and joy. Feeling love for yourself starts balancing the energy not only in your own life, but also your family and friends and co-workers.

Get the grumps and doldrums out of your life, they have no presence or place. Those who moan and whine about everything and everyone have no joy, love or light! They have not opened themselves and have not been touched by Spirit or the Angels. Or the light of the Angels.

Greed has been the downfall of man and an open house for darkness. Everyone loves and wants to follow! Turn your back on greed and move forward into the light. Remember, time and the Angels are on your side. They will show you where you need to go, what you need to know.

When you pray, you talk to Spirit. When you meditate, you are clearing your mind and listening to Spirit. You let Spirit talk to you and give you the answers and guidance you seek. You receive the miracle, the gift, the pleasure of listening directly to Spirit. The messages may be delivered by the Angels, but the words come from Spirit. By meditating daily, you will open a new world to yourself through the Angelic realm. It will lead you on a new life path, seeking all and knowing the answers that are right for you. What a great gift Spirit has given us, knowledge and knowing that life is wonderful and has a purpose. The purpose is to live, learn and love! When you have inner knowing peace, all is as it should be. Let the Angels give you their help. Listen to Spirit and tell many of your experiences. In that way, you are opening many doors so that others can see the light.

We are one with God, we are one with the Angels and we are one with the Earth and Universe. Gather your flock and look Heavenly, for if you look up, down or next to you, whether it be in the stars or here on Earth, you will see Heaven. Feel the warmth of the sun, even in darkness.

Start the healing process and feel joyful for all the many things the Earth and Spirit have provided for your mind, body and soul. Without God and the Angels, where would you be? Could you sustain life? The answer is absolutely not! If you take away what God has given you, all that he has allowed you to have freely, you could not live! You could not breath, you would have no water or food for your body! You would not have a brain to tell you what you need more of, and you would dwindle and die. In fact, you would never have existed in physical form, and you would never have had the opportunity to live on this heavenly Earth! Not without God, His helpers and His messengers. We live and exist through His love, His gifts to us all. Our lives are here, and we are sustained through God and His Angelic realm.

I once had a dream of flying through time and space, flying home to Heaven with the Angels. What a beautiful and busy place to behold, with golden streets and huge buildings of learning.

As I passed through Heaven, everyone was happy and at peace in all ways. Families were lovingly joined. There was no fighting, crime or jealousy and no illness or pain! I saw those who still tilled the soil, still having beautiful gardens, sill fishing from the rivers and still enjoying the best of the life they had here on earth. They were all happy and beautiful, but most of all they were free. Truly free from man and troubles of life here on Earth. They all had true happiness and peace.

I saw embryos of unborn babies that were like stars, floating like balloons with strings attached to couples here on earth and waiting to be born, waiting to give yet more life, learning and understanding to those on this earth.

What a wonderful journey! I was able to truly see the wonders of the Universe and God's home, with his laws taking place in such a beautiful place. Some say what I did cannot be done, but I did it through God and the spirit of openness and love! You must remember, God can do anything. I am only one, but it takes only one to communicate with God and the Angels. You can to if you open yourself to a new realm of possibilities.

Open yourself and believe that there is a much higher power that is greater than yourself out there. By giving and believing in yourself, you are giving and believing in God and His helpers of the Angelic Realm. By opening the doors of knowledge, you open the heart filled with love. By realizing you are a great power, you connect to a greater power. You will take off and zoom to places you never dreamed of going. Open yourself to the unknown, open yourself to God's love through the pathway of the Angels. Have a great trip and transcend from Earth to Heaven and back while flying with an escort of Angels! That gives new meaning to flying "First Class".

Open your channels and receive a wonderful gift of love! Breathe in life and sustain yourself through love and knowledge, giving away your knowledge to help others. Manifesting the little things in life that makes life larger and great, that is what makes life on Earth worth living.

Caring for yourself is caring for others through love, a gift given freely to you from God and the Angelic Realm. Live another day and give another day, sharing all that life has to give back to us. Your life was given to you freely, without judgments or strings. What you choose to do with it is your choice, for it is your life.

Chapter Three

Judgments

One of the most quoted versus from the Bible tells us to "Judge not, least ye be judged." Judgments are something we have been programmed to do since birth. Your parents always expected you to act a certain way or pay the consequences. If you act different from what they expect, you are wrong. You have just been judged.

Abiding by the "Judge not" rule is difficult, especially because it applies not only not judging others but also to not judging ourselves. Aren't most of us our own worst critics? Don't we strive to have more, be more to our communities. Look better and be the pretty one, so others will Envie you. Then you feel you have to act a certain way. And the list goes on from there. How exhausting.

We often set our expectations too high when it comes to others. We cannot expect something of someone else, we must learn to rely only on ourselves and Spirit. For, if others do not fulfill our expectations, then we are let down and go into several emotional states. We feel hurt and anger because we are disappointed that someone did not do as we wanted. All these feelings accomplish is bringing in the negative darkness that covers our light. We become greedy and controlling when we expect so much from others or ourselves. What may be a small thing for you might become impossible for someone else. Quit judging others until you have walked in their shoes.

Being judged and setting limits are different. When limits are set there are boundaries, some good and some bad. However, if you stay in the limits all will be free, allowing you to make the choices. You will have the freedom of choice to do well, be well and act as Spirit would want. What Spirit wants is for you to be you, to find joy and peace in life, not to judge yourself harshly and not to judge others and their acts. For, we do not know their minds or their way of thinking, only they do. What may be wrong for you may be Spirit's perfect way for another individual. Each one of us do things a little different. We all each have lessons to learn and our own crosses to bear.

Until you realize that Jesus will carry your cross, Angels will help carry your burdens. By helping to lighten your load, you will find peace, light and love and you receive your gift! Everything in life has brought you to this moment. You have learned life lessons from all things good and all things bad that have happened to you. Receive the gift and do not ask why, instead ask "What did I learn and what gifts did I receive?"

Get out of the gossip boat that is larger than the Titanic! It is overloaded with passengers, all of them busy talking about and telling their tales on someone else whether the stories are true, false or somewhere in-between. Not only is this a foolish waste of time, but also a very harmful thing to do. You think you are in the know when you gossip! You feel it gives you power and a smug satisfaction. However, when the tables are turned and you are the center of untruths and gossip, what do you feel?

What do those who speak unkindly about someone else gain? NOTHING! Feelings are hurt, anger sets in and even depression for some. This is judging and the boat is sinking. Get out of the boat and focus on positive things. Lighten not only your load but also that of others. Healing starts when you let go of judgments.

The so-called news is another source of gossip and lies that people take for fact. Ask yourself, does the news tell all the facts or just one side? Listen closely and read closely to gain knowledge before you speak. See what is really going on around you before you speak. For to judge falsely is foolish and a waste of life's precious time.

Remember, the tongue is like a sword and can cut sharply or be a beautiful thing. So get off the sinking ship and follow Spirit to dry land. Program your thoughts in a positive and healing way while standing in peace and light with others and within yourself. Use your energy in loving and positive ways and do not speak before you know all the facts. This is knowledge, not hearsay. This is a positive direction, a healthy and healing direction.

You may love someone, but not his or her actions. Remember, they too must walk their own path, learn their own lessons and receive their own gifts. Life is a learning lesson, gaining knowledge to make life easier, not harder! So, let Spirit be the one who judges you and others, you be the one with a clear mind and peace within. You are on your own journey in life. Make your journey a joyful one and leave the judgments and expectations behind. Rise above those who clutter their minds and speak ill of others because you gain nothing for yourself if you stay on their level. Remember, those you gossip with who are telling their stories will eventually get around to talking about you. That is when trouble sets in and anger appears, then you will feel depressed and hurt will take over. Let it go and move forward, move beyond those who have no life and hurt others while they cling to the sinking ship of judging.

The old saying "If you can't say anything nice about someone, don't say anything at all" is what you should always think about. If you do not know the facts, do not tell the story. Hearsay is gossip. It is judging without cause, and it can be slanderous. Do the work and get the facts before you speak and help others in a positive manner versus just talking.

What are just and unjust words? Man will tell you that what they say is justified, where did they receive the information? Where did their knowledge come from? A book? Another man? God, not man, is the one to tell you what is just and unjust, justified or not justified. Go inside yourself by clearing the mind and meditating. Ask God for direction and listen to what he has to say. Listen to your heart of hearts, your gut, then do as God tells you to do and you will not be wrong. You will not wrong another person and your life will be filled with joy and peace.

Man cannot lead you, because he does not know you, your thoughts, your family, your daily life or any of your concerns. Man cannot possibly tell you what will work for you in your life. He cannot, until he is in your place of life at some time. How can he understand and help with what he does not truly know?

So be a free thinker, a free person in life and enjoy being who you are through your God-self. Start by peeling away the layers a little at a time and start healing your mind, body and spirit. Through love of yourself and others, through God.

Master your own life and let others master their own life. This does not mean that you cannot say anything, it just means not to slander or be cruel to someone else or yourself. In other words, again, do not judge. Look in your own mirror before you investigate someone else's. They will have to account for their actions, just as you will have to account for yours, so you had better be ready when the time comes.

Chapter Four

FORGIVENESS

Forgiveness, for those who have sinned against you, is the hardest but healthiest thing you can do. Why? It heals the hurt, anger and fear within you. You do not have to forgive the act, only the person who has harmed you.

When you truly forgive someone, you will instantly feel a relief while a great breath of cleansing escapes along with the pain and any anxiety that has tied you down like a weight. Releasing it and letting go will refresh your life and you will become a healthier and happier person.

Letting go of one of experiences from your past is a very cleansing and healthy act. For example, let's say you were divorced or had an affair with a married man or woman. This event could have happened many years ago, but you still have it stored in your subconscious mind. When you do meet someone who may be the right mate, you are instantly kicked into the boat of swords, cutting this person totally off at the knees before you take a chance. After all, weren't you hurt before, weren't you wronged the last time? This is why forgiveness is so important to your health, both mentally and physically, and to your growth as a human in a spirit form. You must let go of the past through forgiveness to move forward in your life on Earth.

Standing in the light of love, forgiveness becomes easier. Forgive those who have sinned against you, let go of them and move forward on your path of a free and easier life. We all have feelings, and we all have a heart. Hearts Mend! Forgiveness mends the heart, allowing a healthy flow of love and light to all those around you. God leads you to another door of life, in this life, where joy and love are your gifts. The choice is made, and the gift has been received.

Chapter Five

EMOTIONS

Emotions have been imprinted and everything from your past has programmed you. Your family, religion, society and culture have all had an influence. Consciously choose your emotions and thoughts. Recreate yourself and you will have new views, new direction, new focus, new emotions and new experiences. In short, a new life filled with joy and love, taking you beyond and to places you never knew existed.

Some have been programmed not to show true emotions!

You are taught not to cry in public, get angry with someone or even yell when you feel pain. You cannot even smile at the person next to you or show affection in a public place. You are not supposed to have down days and you darn sure shouldn't be happy all the time. Well, let me tell you, if you do not have emotions, good and bad, how will you survive? The drug companies make billions of dollars a year on mood altering drugs. "Just Say No" to drugs! Isn't that what they tell us to do? Most people walk around feeling nothing. They stay in a zombie-like state, until they both wither up and die or they kill someone because the anger and fear consume them.

It is human to show emotion!

If you never know the lows, how can you ever feel the highs in life? If you never cry, how can you feel joy? How can you feel love? Does the sun truly shine on your face or are you a shadow feeling no warmth? How can you think? How do you live? Do you not care about yourself or your life? Do you not care about others? Is this the way Spirit intended you to be? NO!

If we only exist, if we never live, what is the point? To be a puppet on a string, letting everyone else make your decisions? No, that takes your individual rights away. Why would you freely give away those rights? Because you cannot see beyond the darkness. The past drags you down and then you have no future and nothing to look forward to!

If you are that unhappy with yourself and your life, do something to change it. Make the choices that feel right to you. Open your mind to the realm of possibilities that we all have in our lives. Make the Choice!

If you hurt today, make the choice to feel good tomorrow. This truly works. Think of things that make you feel good, such as puppies playing, a beautiful butterfly, a new pair of shoes or maybe your favorite food. Emotions are a good and healthy thing. They make you feel and help you heal. Emotions do need to be controlled, to a point. You do not need to go out and have a screaming fit every day, but you also do not have to suppress all your feelings. Change your emotions to positive thinking. The old saying goes that "an apple a day will keep the doctor away", but so will a smile. A hug definitely will do the trick.

When you feel blue or hurt, call a friend and have lunch. Go visit the sick, elderly or those in a homeless shelter. That will make you feel better. Take a walk and communicate with nature. Get in touch with your Spirit self. Use the left and right side of your brain. For we are Spiritual bodies in human form. Get in touch with your Spiritual self and feel the sun shining on you, even on a cloudy day! The money you spend on drugs, spend on a new dress, or for something, you always wanted.

Can you be happy every day? Yes! When you turn negative into positive feeling, you then can look above a situation, seeing things differently and how they affect you. Put your power to work bringing you out and letting you see. Dream, dare to dream. When you quit dreaming, you quit living. By positive thought, you become a whole and happy person, able to handle the problems in your life.

Feeling good is feeling good about yourself and others. Sharing your knowledge and caring about the knowledge you share.

Balance is the key to life! When you are balanced, you feel good. Things come to you, your choices are clearer, and you are healthier! Focus on your intent, see it, and believe it and it will happen. Open your channels to life and tune in on the good things, not the bad or evil. Stay grounded and become a left, right brain person. Not only feeling emotions, but also experiencing things, you never thought possible.

I am a seer, a channel, one who sees through Gods eyes, and one who helps others through the Angelic Realm. Why? How? Because I believe all things on this heavenly plain are possible. Because I am open to receive, whatever God chooses for me. Because I stay balanced in body and spirit. I am in tune with the universe. With the earth. Simply because I trust and believe in the Supreme being, that created us as brother and sister. I trust the Angels to never be wrong. Foremost I trust and believe in what I do. Healing others! God's plan. What a wonderful and loving gift I have been given.

You have to find your trust, your life. Everyone's different. The plan is individual. How? Through faith and love, through yourself and Spirits love. Today is a great time to begin. This moment. Do not lose another moment in your life. Why? Because when this moment is gone, it will never return. You have lost it. Enjoy the moment and start to feel the emotions, like tides of the ocean, to give you help and release in life. To give you support. Breath in all that you can. Enjoy! Love! Laugh! Dance with the wind and cleanse with the rain. Balance your life and live! Enjoy your new experiences.

Do not bottle up your emotions; they will eventually eat you alive. Creating illness of the mind and body. Emotions are human, they are cleansing, and they are healthy. You should not go around angry or depressed all the time. That is not healthy. Breathe in the positive and exhale the negative. Balance your brain with your heart. Balance your life. Open yourself to new and exciting possibilities! Start by receiving positive help, through Reiki, meditation, exercise, yoga, or simply walking, taking in the beauty that surrounds you.

You think this sounds impossible. Nothing is impossible, when you let Spirit guide you. If you feel you cannot do this by yourself, get a Spiritual healer or teacher to help you. There are many available. They will help you stand solid on the ground. They will not judge you, for the mirror has two faces. They will simply help you start the healing process through yourself. Helping you understand your emotions better and why you feel the way, you do. Clearing your path in life, so that you can move forward into the light of living.

Make the choice and be the positive, powerful person you have hidden within yourself. The choice, of course is yours. Getting lots of vitamin D from the sun is a wonderful antidepressant! 20 minutes in the sun, outside your home, has proven effects on your mental and physical health. If you cannot sleep, get up and exercise, meditate, clean house and soon, you will rest and sleep well. Enjoy the free benefits of health! It is your life, your choice. Take charge of your life and live in balance.

Chapter Six

HOW TO STAY ON YOUR PATH

When you stray off your path, you need to refocus on your intent. Make your intent a priority. Provide each breath with a positive and loving intent. Understand yourself better. Traveling as a whole unit of body, mind and spirit instead of a single unit.

Changing your mind is only a detour, not a good thing to do. Stay on your path and quit letting others pull you off. Listen to your guides and Angels and to yourself. God's child you are, and He will never steer you wrong. Accept your power. Quit hiding it under a refined self. Let it shine when truth is where you are. Do not stumble, for that is when you will fall and disgrace yourself. Be true to yourself and do God's work. It does not matter what others think, say, or feel, for they cannot help but to share your light, when you truly light the beam of your own way, though not only words but also actions.

Throughout the day, live by your life code and not man's, and all you have ever wanted will be yours. The power and the glory of Spirit will guide you to yourself and all things.

Living in the True Light will give you abundance filled with all things.

Let go of those things that are not working for you, and will never work, and walk back to self, and create a wonderful and exciting world. A Heavenly place. A workplace worth working and creating. Go back to the old ways; not to retrace but to journey forward, out of the darkness and negativity, into the light. Recreating your world, shaking it up as an earthquake, to turn over the soil and cultivate what you want in life. It is all there, free to use. Take advantage. Create what you want in life.

Be specific and do good works by living a full life, not just existing.

Release all negativity and those around you who are negative. By doing this, you will live life to the fullest, with laughter, love and joy. Sing and dance away all your fears of the unknown, because there is no unknown, only ignorance of other people.

Chapter Seven

HORRORS THAT WE HAVE
NOT SEEN IN THIS LIFE.

There are horrors that we have not, in this life, seen. Horrors of the mind, flesh and death. Which is worse, to be killed and have darkness of the mind? Or to be killed and have decaying of the flesh? Being aware of all the above helps you and readies you to help yourself and others. The mind and body are tricky places. Blood flows, bloods stops, blood leaks and all for nothing, when the mind has gone on a path to darkness, the body, one way or the other, will soon die. Rather, they are murdered by someone else, or their bodies have been eaten by their minds, and illness (cancer) eats away at them.

Beware of the written contract with God. Those who choose death and dying, either in mind or body, have checked out, only to return and try again. Open your eyes and truly see that death and destruction is all around us! See those people with a different view. They cannot be helped, for they have chosen their way out. By Self Destruction or by the appointed hands of others.

Car accidents, murder, street gangs, wrong diagnosis or losing their minds. Turning a corner, never to be found. You are here and can lead your way to the light, not darkness. Those who consciously choose darkness, leave them behind, and go forward with those who choose to see. Is this you?

Chapter Eight

LIVING IN SPIRIT

Living in Spirit Means Exactly that!

If Spirit heard every thought you had, and every word you spoke, what would you do differently. Guess what, He does. Now if God thought those thoughts and words were prayer? What would you do differently? How would your life be? Would you think differently? Would you speak differently? We all see things differently; we all think differently. The one thing that you know better in this world is yourself. You know things about yourself and your thoughts better than anyone else does. Everything that you think you have hidden within yourself is not so; For Spirit and the Angelic realm knows! You cannot hide even your deepest secrets, wishes, fears, from them. However, they are great secret keepers.

Do not worry you are not being judged. Learn to focus inside yourself, how you feel, how you think and what you speak!

A Loving Supreme Being surrounds us all! Through his love, we are nurtured, grow and live. We are on this Heavenly earth to learn the lessons, receive the gifts and to play. Play is very important, for when we play, we forget the daily stress, all of Life's pressure. Even as adults, we need to dance and touch the earth, you need to find who you truly are! Why you are here, let me tell you, you are here to allow yourself to grow and connect mentally, spiritually and physically.

God gives you freedom of choice. The power of thought, that comes from the mind. Let us all be individuals. Gives you the power to change your lives, your mind, and your thoughts.

He is the Supreme Master of art for he made us all. This earth, the creatures upon it, and the heavenly stars above. Look around you and see, feel the life that surrounds you. The beauty the peace.

Man says to fear God our creator. How can you fear such a loving entity? The creator of all?

Chapter Nine

FAMILY VALUES

WORK, WORK, WORK, IS ALL YOU DO! People, life should not be this way!

Parents have no time for their children. They let machines raise their children impregnating their minds, through the television, computer or the game boy, with violence, fear and negativity.

Family, being the most important thing, you have besides yourself, should be moved forward in your life. Work is a necessary thing; however, when you put your life on hold, consumed by work and getting ahead, letting it be your priority, and your all-consuming purpose, then you have not only neglected you and your soul but also your family and the values of family. When work is ahead of family and yourself, this is wrong.

Our lives are full of worry and unrest! Unrest of the mind. Will this be done today; will I meet my deadline? How can I please my boss, in order to get ahead? Occupying most of our time and space. Cluttering our minds with things that are unimportant. We work for man who tells us these things must be done; we have a deadline, in order to keep our jobs, our lives going. Why? To increase our monetary wealth, to give us more in life and to maintain our lifestyles, to increase our abundance. Our abundance is here and will always surround us, if we let God in and let Him lead us. Sure, we must be able to pay the bills, eat, and live. However, we want more and more. Where is the joy in all of this? What you are creating is Stress!

Heart attacks, strokes, and illness. Is it really worth it? The choice, of course, is yours. We cut our lives short, in order to have more material things. To keep up with the Jones! We neglect our families and ourselves to keep up with man and his rules! I ask you again! IS IT WORTH IT?

By changing a few things in our life and freeing ourselves from the chains of man, we find our God selves and lift the burdens of all things. Through Meditation and prayer, and by turning our concerns, worries over to Spirit, we can literally prolong our lives.

When you smile, your heart opens and stress leaves! When you walk in a flower garden, you feel the beauty and you feel serene. Life does not have to be about stress and worry.

Money is a tool, in which we use to survive. It buys us many things, but it cannot buy your way to God. Only you can find Spirit in yourself. Only you can receive the gift of love.

Life will not go on forever and yet it does. The body will eventually wear out and die but your Spirit, which is energy, will never die. It will find its way back to the beginning. Back to home on a different Heavenly plain. Back to God.

We rush toward nothing when we rush toward man and his rules, his job. In return, we get nothing. We lose our families; our children grow and leave never knowing you. Never feeling your love, never having security from you, they are cold from the machines that have taught them, never having felt the warmth from your touch.

From man we get no joy, no love, only stress and illness. Yet, we allow ourselves to be caught up in this.

Most relationships fail because of money. Not because of love, but money. How sad that we cannot make the choice to love without money. It is the driving force, the rise and fall of all things. There is nothing wrong with having money. God is not opposed to us having money. However, money should not come before family or Spirit! Should not come before joy, or love. Money is a tool of survival and that is all.

Turn to the person next to you and see them as they truly are; See what you find. Most of the time, you will see a sad incomplete human. Why should they be that way when life holds so many gifts?

Because man says we must do this, we must have this, and we must give our time, our energy to him in all things. Times are bad; there is not enough Time; Man is going to do this through you. You are going to follow his rules and do his work. You are going to make him richer. However, is he happy? Probably not.

Man has no warmth, no caring for others. Why is man ill with you doing his work, why is he so stressed? Because, he has not been following God! He too has been programmed by another man. They are ignorant in love; they are programmed to live this way. They need more power, more money, more control. When is there enough?

You have a choice. To turn around and find your God source. To allow peace and joy to come into your life, or to follow the man to where? Darkness? For man cannot get you into Heaven. Only you can get to heaven, for when you go you will travel alone on a well-traveled path. Man does not live your life; you must live your own life. You must stand on your own two feet; you are the only one to walk your own path. No one else can walk it for you. If you fall, you must pick yourself up, no one else can. You must carry your own load, make your own mistakes and learn the lessons and receive the gifts. You must keep a clear path of life. No man can do that for you. Only you can, through your God source.

You know your body better than anyone. You know your thoughts, your aches, pains, and how you feel. No one knows your body and thoughts better than you do. So why do you not take care of something as beautiful and precious as your body and mind. This is yours. Given freely to you by Spirit, not man. You are the one that knows what is best for you. Not man. So why do you not listen to your inner self? Why do you listen to someone else? Take control of yourself. Heal your body and mind and spirt. live this life as you were meant to. You are unique in every way. You are different in every way. You are beautiful and powerful in every way. The choice, of course, is yours. Grow stronger, healthier, and love your body and mind. Use your mind to change your body. To heal yourself, to love yourself.

Start this instant to do what is necessary to become you. The real you! Find out how important you really are, not someone else or who someone expects you to be. Not what others think you should be. Change the programming in your life.

Form a plan and stick to it, you can be anything you want to be. You can become a powerful boss, if you choose to, or you can simply be the baker or candlestick maker. The caring and sharing parent. The choice is yours.

You may just want to be. To be is getting the mind and body at the same place at the same time. Sounds simple but is extremely difficult. Your body may be at work and your mind may be several different places, family miles away, that new dress you have been wanting. Therefore, your mind is entirely somewhere different than your body. Not a bad thing, most people live that way. However, when you clear your mind and focus on putting the mind and body in the same place at the same time, you discover a clear mind and wonderful feeling of joy and love, Just Being! When you do this, you can find out who is walking beside you in your life. Who is helping guide you through this life? Who are your Guides and Angels. Then you find the peace, feeling whole and refreshed. Letting go of fear, because you have found that you are never alone. That you have someone to discuss your life with. To share your burdens. That you have all the help you need. How wonderful it is to know that help is always there, all you must do is ask, and you're Guides and Angels will always answer and help. They are the problem solvers. They hold the answers to all things in this life. They are knowledge, love and joy. They give peace and comfort when you are lost, they will help you find your way when you are sad, they will help you find comfort and joy when you are sick, they will help heal you! What a wonderful gift they give freely to you. They give unconditional love and support whenever you need it. All you must do is ask. All you must do is be open to receive it. Do not turn it away. Open yourself to receive it and feel their presence. You will no longer hunger for more but feel joy in life and live to the fullest. Of course, the choice is yours, to choose your life and to live your life, as you choose. Why not choose a Heavenly life. It may be different from your neighbors, but they are not you! You are special in every way, your own way. That is what being an individual is. So, choose your own destiny, your life and feel this heavenly earth surround you. Letting you go freely in life, unburdened by man, following God's way. Enjoying and changing your work from man's rules to Gods love. See how much easier your day will go. Standing in the light will bring others closer to you in a loving positive way. The choice is yours to be free or chained to man. His rules. Which do you choose? Living life or dying a death in a weak body and mind. Never to have lived, never to have control over your own life. There is only one choice, and that choice is to live a full life, free of chains, free of fear.

MAY THE SUNSHINE ALWAYS ON YOUR DAY!

Chapter Ten

CONNECTING TO THE ANGELIC REALM

Building a bridge to Spirit is like walking across a rainbow. Bright, beautiful colors filled with wonders and miracles you never thought possible. When you communicate with the Angels, messengers of Spirit will guide you across the bright and beautiful sky, to awaken Spirit within you.

I am a seer.

I have seen, and still do see Angels and Spirits. I opened my channels, ready to receive. When you open yourself to new experiences, you will be amazed at what you're capable of doing. By putting aside your fear and darkness, standing in the light. All you have to do is to allow yourself.

#1 you must believe in Angels, and you have to lose the fear of feeling their presence or seeing them.

You need to clear your mind and ask for your Angels and Guides to show themselves or speak to you. (They do all the time anyway.) You just do not realize it. It is as if you are thinking about something and suddenly, this thought pops in your head. You are thinking; where did that come from? Well guess who put that idea or thought in your head. Correct! An Angel or Angels.

You should know that, by first clearing your mind, (not always an easy thing to do for most of us) it will open the channel to the Angelic realm and invite them in. Now remember, Angels do have a unique sense of humor. So do not expect to necessarily see the white winged creatures of the universe. They can appear as they choose fit. Sometimes in a monk's robe or they can appear as blue, red, green, yellow, gold, purple Angels, you just never know. They sometimes come immediately; however, they do love to surprise you.

I came home one day from doing some Spiritual work, opened my front door and there in my living room, stood this Huge Angel. I was startled and squeaked OH! That Angel did a little dance, he was so happy! I knew, of course, that it was Cerviel. Now Gabriel likes to peek around corners and surprise me from time to time. Mary is always so loving and appears in different ways, usually hooded in lavender, holding a shaft of wheat.

No matter how they appear, you will love their presence. You must thank them for they love praise.

They are with us all. Find out who your Angel's are and that Angel's purpose in your life. They may not all appear at once but, in time, they all will dance around you, surrounding you with love. There is no better hug than from an Angel's wing.

They want to help, so do not hesitate to ask for guidance and assistance in all things. It makes things so much easier for you. Be specific, when you ask them for assistance. I have not, a time or two, and got exactly what I asked for. Missed directions. They think that's hysterical!

I find other people's Angels and Guides. It's really a simple process for me because I let my Angels do the work. I simply ask mine to go, find yours. They love doing this. It's almost like a game for them, in which they win! When we all win!

Angels are Omni present, which means, they can be in more than one place at the same time. So, you may have the same Angel as I do, however, you may live across the world from me.

By opening your channel and connecting with your Angels, you have opened your heart to trust and feel love. You have opened a large part of your God Spirit connection. Angels give you evidence that there is a place beyond this earth. That there is help out there. That you are truly never alone. That is something larger than we are to believe in.

Earth is a heavenly place, an extension of Heaven, where we live in physical form. Our energy is what connects us to Spirit, Friends and Family, called Angels. Invite them in, for they travel this life with you. They are your personal tour guides, assistants and knowledge-able beings. For they can help you find the answers that are right for your path.

When you open your Angelic channel, others start opening and propelling you forward in the light of happiness and wholeness.

Chapter Eleven

Experiences in Life

Every day you gain more knowledge, more wisdom. Every day someone else enters your life, from which you learn. It can be the checkout girl, mail carrier, and a person driving by you on the road. Briefly, they all tell you something. They may be a hard worker, angry, lazy, beautiful, whatever it is you have gained some knowledge from that person. Your brain stores that knowledge for you. Your body reacts to that knowledge. Example: If you are driving down the road and an angry driver fly by you honking their horn, shaking their fists at you, your reflexes take over, after the brain says, "look out". You immediately jerk awake and are ready to move your car. Emotions run from fear to anger at a person you have never seen. They have put you on alert. They have given you some type of reaction. You will likely never see that person again, but they have given you another experience in life. You go home and tell your family about this experience. Perhaps not knowing why that person was so angry with you.

Sometimes you receive kindness from a stranger. Example: Your child gets lost in the grocery store and someone brings that child back to you, filling you with relief, handing your, unharmed, child back to you with a smile of love. All these experiences are helping you to grow inside. Opening doors, you did not know were closed, creating different emotions.

If you never know the lows in life, how would you ever know the highs? Life is full of peaks and valleys, when you are on the peaks, life is wonderful, riding you higher and you feel lighter and higher. However, when you are in the valley, darkness rules, you become sluggish. These are called life cycles. We all have these times, for we are all human. It is what we do to keep ourselves out of the valleys of life that counts.

The one thing you must do is keep moving forward in life. Through prayer, meditation and positive thinking you will rise back again to the peak of life. One thing I do, when I am having a valley day, is say aloud, "Thank you God for a wonderful day and a wonderful life". I immediately feel the weight being lifted, the darkness disappearing and the light stars shining through. Then I can turn all my troubles over to the angels. I release them for the angelic realm to take care of. Everything turns out exactly as it should and done with ease. Then life is a breeze. If the wind blows too strong, you can bend with it. Be more flexible in life. Ride the storm out and receive the gift at the end, a beautiful clear sky, lighting the earth, making colors clean and bright. This is how life is. Remember, darkness turns to light in your mind. All you have to do is see the light to all things around you. For you to are a powerful being

There is a negative and positive to all things. You cannot start your car if the battery cable is off on the negative side.

The key is balancing the negative and positive energy. Again, the highs and lows of life. Use the negative as a balance for the positive. Use it as a grounding tool. To center and relax you, you use the positive side to lift you up higher and lighter. It is all an illusion, but necessary to maintain balance in all things. Sometimes called the yen and yang of life. Controlling the negative and positive is turning the wheel of balance. Making the negative an advantage, instead of lowering and darkness Use it as a tool to ground, to relax and to invigorate and store energy. Therefore, you can be positive and feel healed. Letting go of stress, healing the mind, body and spirit. Isn't negative and positive great! Spirit shows us a fuller life. The great being He is.

Chapter Twelve

THE SWORD
10/12/2005

If someone gave you a sword, what would you do with it? Would you pick it up and start chopping people's heads off, cutting them off at the knees? Or would you lay the sword down and walk over it, standing in the light, see it as a beautiful object, with many different uses? It is shiny and has a carved handle.

Our tongue is like a sword, sometimes we use it to speak in haste, unpleasant, hateful words, or we use it to speak loving words.

Have compassion for others, have passion for yourself. Think about the effects your words have on someone else. If a mother tells a child, you are ugly, or if a mother tells a child, you are beautiful; what effect do those words have on that child? An everlasting effect, either way.

Just take a moment, stop and think before you speak. Are your words, your thoughts positive or negative? Remember, the tongue is like a sword and can be a useful tool, or a beautiful tool. Which will your tongue be? The choice, of course is yours.

Chapter Thirteen

MONEY AND ABUNDANCE

Monetary abundance is something you cannot force. You must put out there that you are flying and picking money up off the ground. We all can be money magnets. We all need money to sustain living arrangements, pay bills.

When you say that you are poor, then you become poor. You may be without enough monetary abundance, but never say I am poor. You are not poor; you just do not have enough cash for today. You must decide, how much is enough? Is a $1,000.00 or $10,000.00 enough? You then must send your monetary Angels out for what you need. Follow your gut, and then take the opportunity to make money and more money.

Money often comes in strange ways. Be open to receiving money.

Drop the financial quicksand, in other words, quit saying that you are poor, or I will never have the money I need! You have everything you need and then some.

The first thing you have to decide is to be sure and get paid money for the work that you do. I know there are times you are not paid enough for you to survive. You are just happy to be able to do something you love doing or perhaps you do not have enough confidence in your ability. For your services, start being paid what you are worth. Everything you do is worth something. Do not give away the store but treat your business like a business. Treat yourself as someone worthy. Praise is always uplifting when you do a good job for someone; however, money pays the bills and keeps us going. Do not give your services away.

Use the left side of your brain to receive money, and the right side to use money wisely.

If you see a penny on the street, do you stop and pick it up? Well start doing that. Most people will not, why, because it is not enough. You would really be surprised how many pennies I find a day. Especially in a shopping mall or theater. When you pick that penny up you must thank God for your abundance. For pennies make dimes and so forth. Just remember to keep it coming with positive thinking and attitude.

Remember, you never fail at anything, you just learn another lesson. At the end of that lesson, you receive the gift of knowledge. How to do things better the next time.

So, keep your monetary abundance coming, thank God for your abundance and ask for the abundance you want.

Chapter Fourteen

THE WONDERS OF LIFE

There are many wonders in this life. The Taj Mahal, Pyramids of Egypt, Eiffel Tower, London Bridge, and many more, some man made, and some created by Spirit. We all know and recognize all the above, but what about simple everyday wonders in this life. A newborn child, holding a small puppy, loving someone, a beautiful flower, or a gentle loving note from a friend. A child's drawing. All wonders of life and all beautiful.

The oceans have a life that lives in deep waters, mountains that are majestic, beautiful and alive.

When I hear someone say that God has never given them a miracle, I ask if they have ever looked around them and seen a butterfly, a hummingbird, a bumblebee. How wondrous these things are. All different in their own way. All making us seem small in the scheme of things. All perfect and as they should be.

I live on a farm and see nature at work every day. Creating more and more beauty on this earth. Living creatures, wondrous things, a newborn fawn, small playful foxes. A turtle that is solid and consistent. Playful rabbits, a quail that can fly and the hawks that talk to us as they hunt and fly. These too are wonders of the world; these too are miracles that Spirit has created. They are constantly at work and constantly at play. They give me strength, energy, love and support. I have seen bear claiming a small pine tree and how he labors to get where he is going. Cougars slinking and thinking they are hiding from view, all with grace and beauty.

How do these wondrous things differ from humans? NOT at all. We all, even the animals, strive to get ahead, strive to hide from view, and strive to survive in this world.

Why, when some create their world, they cannot live in it? They cannot survive in what they have created for themselves.

For some, change is fearful. However, if you created it, why not just change it? Because they do not know how, and fear presents itself. The unknown can be fearful, can be challenging.

It is so simple to change the world you created; simply walk away from it. Start creating a new world. Don't worry what others think. Change can be great. You can be great, happy and at peace. Simply by being the wonderful, powerful person you were meant to be. Follow your dream on a star and standing solid in your new wonderful world!

Through Spirit and the Angels!

Chapter Fifteen

TIME IS PASSING BY

Tick, tick, tick, hurry, hurry, hurry. Time is passing us by, and we cannot catch up. Life is slipping away a little at a time. You don't have enough time for any joy or relaxation in your life. You're a parent, employee, and child. You have responsibilities and duties.

Well, not all is as it may seem. First, you have all the time in the world and then some, second, you have choices. One including turn off your television, computer, phone and use that time (approximately 2 hours a day) to discover a new and beautiful you. Relax; all is as it should be.

Surprises are a good thing and in life you may be surprised to find out you're a Powerful being, beautiful and pure, calm and serene. Even Loving.

So, stop the clock and do something for You. Sit by the fire and read, meditate, light a candle or soak in the tub. Breathe! Most forget to breathe during their life.

You hunger for a peaceful, quiet life. You want for and look for joy, love, and roses. Where are they? They are everywhere when you open yourself, when you love yourself, when you look around you, when you stop being someone besides yourself. Most people do not have a clue who they really are.

You were given a heart, to listen to it beat, the rhythm, the sound so soft; this is the place of love! Open your heart and love all things, especially yourself. You were given a brain (The using Tool) to think and learn, to understand things. Why do you not use it for yourself? Why only use one side when you have two sides? By combining the heart and mind, you can do anything you set out to do through love and knowledge! Use what you have stored.

You were given a body to house all that you are. Accept that body and take care of your body. Enjoy the body (or housing) you were given. By combining the heart, brain (or mind) and body; you are complete in a small but powerful unit. How divine you are. How totally perfect you are. How powerful you can be.

We, as humans think less than most animals. We can't make our own decisions. We must have someone else tell us what we should do, how we should think. Animals tend to run together for companionship. However, watch as one decides to do something different. They just turn and are gone in another direction. Making that decision. No one told them what direction to take or when to take it.

You will never know how much power you have, unless you use it. You'll never know true love, unless you open your heart. You will never have knowledge, unless you think for yourself. Do not close these life essentials down. Open and combine them all.

Squirrels gather nuts for winter; we gather knowledge for another time. When we need it.

What this is telling you is to have faith in yourself. Quit putting your faith, your life, in someone else's hands. Quit listening to man who has no faith and lots of false power. Use your power and you will have true faith! It all comes from within. The heart and the brain; Housed by your body. Created by God, not man. Open and listen to yourself and find out what gifts you have. Find your own source through God. Live Life and quit going through the motions. Wake up each morning feeling refreshed, energized. Sunshine and roses; even in winter. Music and laughter throughout your day. Giving you a gift from Spirit, A great, happy and wonderful life.

41

Chapter Sixteen

IMAGINATION

Imagination is a wonderful thing to have. Without it where would we be? How would we live? Look around you at the tall buildings, the automobiles we drive, even the foods we eat. Without imagination, none of these things would happen.

Imagination, vision, or purpose is all the same. Use your imagination to re-create yourself, your world.

By using our minds in a positive enlightened way, we journey forward creating a world of beauty. When you imagine that you are floating on a beautiful white cloud, then you relax the mind and body, feeling at peace.

If you imagine that you can walk tall and feel great, chances are you will. If you imagine that you are a success at your job or in your life, then you will be.

You will not necessarily build buildings or design automobiles; however, through your imagination you can build and create a beautiful space and life, especially for you. Surrounding you with the love and peace you seek.

Center yourself and let your imagination work for you in a positive, loving way. Do not hesitate to move forward on what you imagine in your life.

Our minds are powerful, creating our thoughts, directing our actions. So, use your mind to create all you want in this life.

Imagine yourself well and whole, at peace with all things in your life. Living harmoniously with all of God's creation. One step brings you higher, to a greater awareness. Opening your imagination to create more wealth in your life, more joy.

Let your imagination run free and enjoy the ride of creation, life and positive living.

Chapter Seventeen

VACATION OF THE MIND

A vacation of the mind is a wonderful thing! Especially when stress seems to be leading all other thoughts. Sometimes we just need to escape and go somewhere. When it's not always possible to leave work, and home physically, you can leave anytime mentally.

Set the mood by lighting incenses or candles. Don't forget to turn off your television and phone. If you want to go to the beach, lie on your favorite beach towel and turn on your favorite beach music. Now lay back and focus on a day at the beach.

When you relax and take a vacation of the mind, no matter where you go, you'll come back feeling refreshed and revitalized.

You can also have others join you on a vacation of the mind, by having friends over for an indoor picnic or bar-b-que. If your vacation is in the mountains, have friends over for a ski lodge party. Decorating your home as if it were your favorite vacation spot. Vacationing can be a year-round experience and not just for a few days.

Try this and see how wonderful vacations can be. No planes to catch, no packing, just relaxing and putting stress aside, just having fun! Feel the warmth of the sun and enjoy.

Chapter Eighteen

THE ANTICHRIST HIDES SO WELL

There has not been another time in history where the Antichrist has been able to hide so well.

From the beginning of time, we have been faced with the battle of Christ and the Antichrist. Then, the Anti-Christ was seen as what they were. Now they hide in Christ's name so well. We, the true believers in God, see them everywhere.

They say, "Follow me and ye shall find." Find what? Fear, hate, loss of freedom, jealousy, a world of darkness. Waiting to tell you what to do, when in your heart you know what is right and what is wrong. Just because someone else follows does not mean you have to. Listen to your God self and make your own choices.

I could not live in that world. So, I chose light, Love, peace and happiness! I follow no man, nothing except God and his world. Where earth is filled with Heavenly things for me. Where peace and love reigns over darkness and Hellish nightmares.

The Antichrist is so well hidden in rich suits, fine cars, big homes, calling you to look and see what you, too, can have. Giving more money to them. To buy what? Money will not buy a place in Heaven. All you must do is what they say. They control you by fear and greed. They cannot see, for they do not know. They say let's fight our neighbors, lie, when the truth is better, let's have unrest (for if you rest you may find a better way. Peace). Yes, the Antichrist does not show you, their horns. But they are there. They are just hidden.

Look at all those around you who are suffering from illness, depression, unhappiness, feeling unloved or anger, you have a choice.

Don't wait too long, standing in the love of Christ under an angel's wing of protection, the only protection we need. The Antichrist cannot face God! They cannot feel love or give love. It's up to you to know the difference. Challenge them with your power of Love and Light. They will turn away and run from you. They cannot stand the light. They will disappear before your eyes.

Our creator was God! Our healer is God; our truest form of prayer comes from God! Won't you join the fight and battle against the Antichrist? All so easily done, simply open your heart, and arms, and welcome God into your life. Forget about getting ahead of others but walk side by side with your relations, help them to find the light. You do not have to be armed with a gun or knife, only with the light of the life you walk.

Clear your path of obstacles and hurdles by stepping over them. Tear down the signs that say anger, fear and hate live here. For your sign should read; all that enter here stand in the light of glory and salvation. Welcome to my life. See you on the other side. Of lightness.

Yes, the Antichrist is here and among us all, don't be afraid to be free, and overcome the Antichrist who is trying to control your mind, body and spirit. Walk away from the greed of man.

The Heat will melt them down, while you fly away to a heavenly place. Taking a seat next to Jesus of Nazareth by the Red Sea. That is Jerusalem the new way. Shedding darkness to stand always in the light of day. How wonderful it is to experience New Beginnings! Being whole.

When the rain falls and the wind blows, it brings us cleansing down deep in the core of things. This choice is yours as to how to clean it up. All you have to do is start. A little at a time and soon all will be well. Health over illness, joy over fear, love over hate. AS IT SHOUD BE!

Let the Antichrist cry out in pain when you stand in God's Love, everlasting. Yes, we fight. We can win this battle of evil and darkness, by following our hearts and letting God the Spirit lead the way.

Chapter Nineteen

THE LADY BUG

I had a ladybug land on my dining room table, upside down. She lay there, struggling to get right side up, without any success. I could see the life going right out of her. I, very gently, turned her over and still she did not move. I then took my finger and, ever so gently, touched her. Still no movement. So, I then put my finger just above her and let the energy from Reiki run, for a very few minutes. She soon began to switch her wings and soon she began to crawl, as she felt the life force energy going through her. What an amazing thing to see.

Do we not all get upside down in life from time to time? We struggle and struggle to get where we need to be, or to be turned over, or around, and nothing seems to work? However, when we quit struggling and let the energy of the universe flow, things seem To start moving in the right direction. Turning us over and letting us to kickstart your heart and mind. To fly away from trouble. Bringing us closer to our accomplishments. Redirecting our energies to positive instead of negative. Allowing us freedom of thought. Clearing the way and giving us more inner choices.

The nicest thing about universal energy is it is free! You will never have to buy it and it never runs out. You will have all you ever need.

Therefore, the next time you feel as if you have been flipped over on your back, and the life is going out of you, and trouble is all around you, Ask God for the energy to turn yourself over and start the day new. Allow yourself to feel energized, breathe in the energy to kick-start your heart and mind. Never to look back at the trouble, but to look at the intent of now and how you got there alive, energized and living a life in the light.

There is no need to struggle in life. Feel your passion and go for the positive. Your energy, like the Ladybug's, will soar.

Chapter Twenty

MESSENGERS

The Angelic realm are wonderful messengers! They work for not only Spirit but are here for you. Let them help take you to a world of peace and tranquility. Let them deliver the message of Spirit, that he has for you. Let them guide you on your life path, lighting the way for you. You must open yourself to all possibilities in this earth life. They will propel you to the end. Creating a new more wonderful life for you. Letting your light shine, leading you to peace through God's love and protection. Paving the way for you, helping you become the powerful being Spirit meant you to be. Freeing you from the chains of man and man's control. Freeing you from anger, suffering and showing you the positive side of living a full life. Isn't that what you are looking for? Love, joy and peace. Find peace within yourself, through the Angels God provides for you. They love to be used. They love to work, and the best part is they are free. They cost you nothing and in turn, they will free you. They will free you from the chains of restraint that others have placed on you.

One thing you can count on is never having to be alone, for Spirit will never leave you, Angels will never leave their post of protection. A person can be lonely in a crowd of people, or a person can feel comfort standing alone. Which do you choose to be? God is a great source of peace, love and holding a light for you to see your way out of the darkness.

Following a bright shining star. Feeling the heavenly bodies surround you with peace, comfort and love. Allowing you to fly freely from darkness into the light of living. For if you sustain life, you become whole and one in body, mind and spirit.

Learn how to communicate with all things in this life. Communicating with the Angelic realm and Spirit, opens a world book of knowledge, creating a wealth of the mind. Letting you actually feel! Most people do not feel. They only are like robots and do as they are programmed to do. If they do start to feel, then someone gives them a pill to level things out. You have to know the lows in life in order to feel the highs. You must experience life. You are an individual, and your mind works independent of anyone else's on this earth. USE IT! Do not close your mind to the possibilities in this life. Be open to all things and everyone who knocks on your door.

Chapter Twenty One

THE RIGHT OF PASSAGE

Who gives you the right of passage? Does man, who condemns all worldly acts, or does God? Man says, "If you do what he says, you will enter the kingdom of heaven. (You will gain the Right of Passage". God says, "All who believeth in Me will have ever-lasting life." Therefore, if you believe in God, or Spirit, or whatever you choose to call the Supreme Being, then you have been given the Right of Passage. It makes no difference what man says. No man has the power that Spirit has. No man can foretell what God is thinking. For God will not let you slip away, if you truly believe. Clinging to the rock of man will not give you the Right of Passage. However, letting go of man; being free from the rock to flow through life peacefully and happy, following the laws of living, created by God and only God, will give you the Right of Passage! Standing only in the light of Spirit. Obeying God and loving your God self. Not to fear God or the unknown, but to welcome them into your life, your being. You do not need someone else to tell you who you are and what you need to do to find peace in the love of Spirit!

The world rotates and spins on its axis, always changing, never sitting still. We, as humans are the same way. We are always changing, never sitting still. Some are never grounded or settled. They have a restless soul, so they also have a restless mind. Why? Because they cannot see, they live in fear and fear creates anger, making us needy, making us doubt ourselves, then no one can move forward, only sit in their chair and spin in circles of darkness. Are you still in the darkness or do you stand in the light? Do you fear all things and Spirit, or do you trust in Spirit to lead you?

Open your eyes and see what is truly going on around you, within your home. Amazing how when we see those in darkness, non-believers who we say have no Right of Passage. We cry for others, who will never know true joy or love in their hearts. All we see is greed and clinging to man's rock of pain. Waiting to see if they will ever let go.

Letting go is like flying through space and time toward the stars and heaven. Like free falling in space and time. Feeling relaxed and happy, a true smile comes to your face and peace within. Why? Because being is all you, have to do. Believing in Spirit is all you have to do to gain the Right of Passage.

Ask God and you; too, shall receive all good things in life. Your abundance will overflow. Your health will improve, and Life will be good.

If those who cling to the rock of man throw stones, forgive them for they do not know. How can they, when man says it is wrong? They have not seen, and they are ignorant in their life of darkness. Forgive those who do not know. Let them see your light of inner peace and happiness. They can choose to cling to the rock of man or gain the Right of Passage to everlasting life. A life with a heavenly purpose, a life of love, filled with joy and peace. The choice, of course, is yours. Don't wait too long, time slips by us quickly and silently. We enter this world with nothing, and we will leave with nothing; save the lessons we have learned and taking with us the gifts from the lessons. The mind is a precious gift, do not waste it. Use it to store the knowledge and gifts for those left behind, so they too can have the Right of Passage. Therefore, they too, can have the Glory of God. What a wonderful world we leave behind, entering a place of peace and love, to live in our natural state of Spiritual being. Sitting at the foot of God. To tell Him of our learning's here on earth. An extension of Heaven. Bear in mind that you cannot serve two masters. Not man and God, but only truly God. For God gave you the breath of life. Man just lets you see the other side of life, the human side, and man brings you to darkness; Man controls the actions you make, the money you make, where you stand in society. Man is measuring you by the house you live in, the money you make, not what is in your heart. God accepts you as you are. God lets you light your way, to see all life has to offer. Decide now on where you stand, time is truly passing you by.

Do not judge man, for it is God who will be the judge. We are not the jury; we are not wise enough to look into man's hearts and minds. We do not know what prompts their actions. Only God knows. So sit down your sword, and breathe in the positive, exhale the negative, giving those around you the breath of life. Again, only God has the power over all of us. He has a plan for every one of us. What is yours? Listen through meditation and let Spirit advise you. Only He can judge! Only Spirit can grant the Right of Passage.

Chapter Twenty Two

JUST A LITTLE LIGHT

As I set in a meadow, listening to the water stream over the rocks, I look above at the Snow Peak Mountains. I feel the presence of God and the Angelic realm surrounds me. Giving me strength of conviction. Feeling the warmth and love from all things, the earth and the heavenly bodies. Just Being. How wonderful and beautiful the quiet awe is. An eagle cries and I receive the message that we all can soar higher in our spiritual bodies. Letting go of everyday stress, fear and finding peace.

God's presence allows us all.

What a magical and wonderful place this earth is. Staying grounded yet flying higher than we have ever been. Come, won't you sit with me and enjoy just being who you really are. Traveling with the mind, body and spirit as one.

Chapter Twenty Three

A WELL TRAVELED PATH

Journey is never ending but everlasting. From birth, we travel a path to take us back home, to our heavenly home, where God resides, and man is just a helper. Some are chosen and some dismissed to return.

Those who are lost and do not believe will travel a cluttered path in life, a path leading nowhere. Taking them deeper into darkness, away from the heavenly light. In darkness grows fear and anger, greed consumes them. Jealousy becomes their bride. All creating illness of the mind, body and spirit. Eating away all love and peace, consuming them until they can no longer see or find their path. They become cold as stone.

God shines a brilliant light on those who are willing to follow his path and stand in his footsteps. Standing in a light that holds peace, love and healing energy, opening your eyes to all things. Opening your heart to love, allowing you to see beyond yourself, beyond man, bringing you higher to fly to God's side and feel His warmth, His love. Making you whole and all things possible in your life. Mending the open wounds, clearing the vision to see beyond, allowing you to speak in a positive loving way. Healing the body and letting you feel the joy of the earth. The sun that shines in the morning, a gentle rain of spring. A beautiful snow filled morning. Sitting by the fire on a cold evening or swimming in the lake on a hot summer day. The horizon, as the sun sets at the end of the day. All of these, the miracles created every day by God's hand. The divine master, the supreme artist who created a beautiful world. A world in which man has polluted; the air, the water, cut the beautiful timber, to replace it with asphalt. Man has bombed the earth, dug into the earth, drilled in the earth and built mansions to reach the sky and block our view of heaven. To surround us with nothing. All in the name of progress.

He fills us with pills and tells us help is on the way. Never arriving! Almost here but never quite near enough to help. Never on time.

We can send men to the moon but cannot feed the many starving in this world. Man isolates you from all things bad, only to destroy you when you overstep your boundaries. Not God's boundaries, but man's. When you dare to think outside the box. When you dare to speak your true thoughts. When you dare to act as a free individual, well, we are all individuals and each of us is perfect in our own way.

By standing in God's light and staying on your Spiritual path you will find peace, light and warmth. Unconditional love of oneself and love for others. Lifting you above others, lightening your load, propelling you farther in your life. Letting you see the whole of things, not just a speck of things.

God created the greatest masterpiece when he created you. He gave you life. He molded you in his image. He will heal you and protect you, if you are willing to accept his love. All you have to do is quit fearing God and accept God's love. How easy! Yes, life should be easy, full of joy and love. Beauty surrounds you, enjoy it. Take a walk and really look around you. Look at the many colors that surround you, and then look up at the blue sky, the radiant sun, and the beautiful stars that guide you through the night. Listen to the quiet and see what you hear. Nothing? Listen to your heartbeat, the wind in your hair, and your footsteps in the sand. Created all for you. Miracles of life! Miracles of love! Given to you freely from Spirit.

The choice, of course, is yours. Open your mind and connect your heart, to become the powerful person you were meant to be. Live life to the fullest and gain your right to be alive. Life over death, because at the end we are all going home. Do it right this time around. Believe in God's supreme presence in your life and feel his supreme love. Trust in His wisdom of all things. For He can move heaven and earth. He can part the seas and He can walk on water. Listen and you too can hear the ocean, in such a small thing as a Seashell. Miracles do happen every day. A dew drop feeds a leaf. Let God feed you.

Chapter Twenty Four

ANGELS NEVER LEAVE

One thing you can count on is never having to be alone; for Spirit will never leave you, Angels will never leave their post of protection. Even if you betray them, send them away, they will not go far and will await your call. You may think you have sent them away, but all you have to do is ask the Angelic realm for help and guidance, and they will be there for you, all you have to do is be open to receive them.

A person can be lonely in a crowd of people or feel comfort alone. Which do you choose to be? God is a great source of peace, allowing you to feel love and holding a light for you to see your way out of the darkness.

By following a bright shining star, feeling the Heavenly bodies surround you with peace, comfort and love. Allowing you to fly, free from darkness and into the light of the living, the light of life. For if you sustain life, you will heal and become whole in body, mind, and spirit.

Chapter Twenty Five

THE SEVEN CANDLES

Line up seven candles and light them all at the same time. All will burn, some burning more brightly. Some slower, some faster, some will not hold a flame at all. When the flame lowers and burns slower, a darker shadow will appear, and when the flame burns out, total darkness surrounds an empty stand.

When your mind is in darkness, you, too, are an empty shell. No light or flame burns within you, you stand in total darkness. Not able to think or move on your own, someone must come into the darkness and led you around. However, when the flame burns brightly it lights your way, showing you the direction to take. Directing your energies in a positive way. Darkness creates fear. Seeing everything as the unknown, creating more fear. Anger then sets in, and you have no true reality of feeling, of the things around you. Your energy drops and depression sets in. Moving becomes impossible. You cannot sit, you really cannot move for being frozen in fear. This is not living. This is not what life was meant to be.

By lighting one simple candle, a small flame will help you see your way to the door and out of the room, which holds you hostage. Helping to lead you to your path of living. You will feel the warmth from a single flame. The choice, of course, is yours. You can discover your light and reclaim your life, or you can go on living in darkness with fear and anger. Darkness creates dampness and mold! Cold! After a while it will create illness of the body, penetrating the mind.

When more than one flame is lit, you feel real warmth and secure in the light. Relaxing as you move forward in your life. Confident about choices. The inner flames start fueling the mind and body. Energy returns, colors are brighter and seeing what is ahead is not obstacles; it is no longer a chore to move. The flame within surrounds you and lights the way ahead of you. You are no longer frozen in time. What a wonderful gift. Truly living as God meant you to. When one energy candle lights, it will spontaneously light the other six. Showing you a brighter light. Opening all the blocks of the body, mind and spirit. Thinking becomes clear, action and movement are more fluid (like a dancer on a stage) letting you move gracefully forward in your life, a stronger more positive being. You then become more beautiful with time, and the rhythm of things. Joy fills your heart and love is felt. Not only toward others but also for yourself. Now the dance of life has truly begun. You can waltz through life or fast dance through. The choice is yours. Yours only. Finding your way out of the darkness is the hard part; letting yourself live without fear. The easy part is living in the light, letting your candles burn brightly.

Make the choice to be your own person, a free living, loving, human being.

Opening the chakra's, the energy systems of life, one grounding you, one letting the sexual and creative center open, one letting you feel love, one opening the throat and allowing speech, one seeing the unseen glory of the universe and one letting you think. Letting the energy run through the body as a healing tool. By balancing the chakras in the body, and opening the systems of the body, you are then healing your mind, body and spirit. The main thing is to keep moving forward on your path. Do not let man detour you and drag you back into darkness. Hold your head up and square your shoulders move forward on your life path. Do not let your mind get cluttered with ifs but keep focused on your intent. You are what you intend. You will then start to prosper, in many ways. Life is full of abundance and gifts; receive them graciously.

However, Darkness is always waiting, by looking up instead of down; the light will always be with you. In life, we have everything we need and then some. We have all the tools for life we need.

The choice is yours. Will it be light days or dark days? Will you know and experience Spirit in your God self or will you know or experience nothing? Only to know what someone tells you to feel. Will you feel peace and love, or will you feel anger and hurt? Again, the choice is yours. Fulfilling your contract with God and His purpose for your existence is the greatest joy you will have in your life. Remember, you are a Powerful Being, now is the time to start using the power we all have within us.

Chapter Twenty Six

BUILDING A BRIDGE IN YOUR LIFE

Building a bridge in your life is like stretching the imagination between earth and the universe. Connecting with Spirit, the bigger than life identity from within. Staying connected with the positive that surrounds you and is here for you to grab hold of though opening the heart and freeing the mind of all worries, fear and stress.

By caring for yourself on the inside, balancing your energies, feeling peace, and connecting with your Spirit self, you become a radiant, beautiful human. Acknowledge your Spiritual being and embrace life. Be the powerful person, you were truly meant to be. Though God's love, you will expand your horizons, your thoughts become focused. Your brain is awakened, and your vibrational level will lift you higher in this life. Let go of old habits, addictions, compulsions, and negative thoughts.

When you feel God's touch and surround yourself with the Angelic realm, you feel Gods presence, you become knowing of the universe and earth. You will then feel complete. No drug can make you feel this way, and the amazing thing is you will keep on feeling this way, no matter what happens in your life, for you have found peace and the true meaning to life.

You do not have to listen to man and his negative words. Listen to only positive love, and happiness.

Then you have truly achieved what it is to never be alone. To never have trouble sit on your doorstep. Then you have become an individual, living and breathing in the positive. You will not listen to those who want to drag you back into darkness with their stories of discontent. For those things are unimportant compared to the understanding and good for all things.

When you heal and feel good, you will start to take positive steps toward looking good. It will no longer be a chore to take better care of yourself. You will no longer hide under an affliction of being too heavy, thin, plastic surgery, and taking pills to feel better. Because you are better, you will have more energy! Because you will see your life in a positive, powerful way. By eating healthy, exercise, a new youthful you will emerge.

Keep the wheel turning, keep it greased, and keep it moving in the direction you want to go. Some others have no life, so they live through yours, drawing and directing your life and what you did or did not do, because they are not brave enough to stand on their own, but have to live someone else's life dragging your energy down, your health down. Fear holds them, like a chain around their necks. They are frozen, cannot move away from the darkness of fear. They do not trust in Spirit, and they do not trust themselves.

Though my book, you have gained knowledge, you have been given love, for I write this book though love of the Supreme Being and the Angels.

To look younger and more beautiful, you must feel younger and beautiful! You have to do the work; you have to play and take in all that life gives you. You truly must start feeling! Positive feelings!

When trouble heads your way, ask God to intervene. Believe that He will, and He will. Believe in miracles, believe in love, and believe in yourself! All is there for the taking. All is there waiting for you to let go and believe!

Life can start new and fresh, this very second. Remember to keep your feet on the ground and your heart soaring. Take a deep breath and thank God for this day, this life He has given you.

· Then you must be ready to cross this bridge in life and move forward! Connecting to all things seen and unseen in your life. Accepting yourself as you were meant to be. Having faith in Spirit.

Remember, we are individuals not designed to be a clone of someone else! Not meant to be a Twiggy! When you are so insecure that you pay more and more money to stay young and beautiful, you have not learned the lesson. You cannot share the love of others, because you cannot build your body and face on false idols.

Don't those models in the magazines look perfect? Doesn't everyone want to look like them, be like them, and wear clothes like them? Not all that glitters is gold! Therefore, accept who you are and enjoy life around you. Get outside and breathe, stop and smell the flowers, enjoy the garden, for our bodies are like a beautiful garden, it needs to be tended to each day and occasionally, a weed or two may need to be pulled!

Enjoy this Heavenly earth and a universe filled with wonder and miracles of the stars. Most of all, stand on your bridge and enjoy being you.

Chapter Twenty Seven

REBECCA'S METAPHYSICAL MOMENTS

When you pray to talk to God or a supreme being. When you meditate, you open yourself to let Spirit talk to you.

When you stand in Spirit's footprints, you are no larger than the smallest grain of sand. When you receive love, through Spirit, you become larger than life.

Live life to the fullest on this Heavenly earth. Touch someone in need and feel love, like a gentle rain.

Seeing through one's mind's eye is like looking into the beyond.

We all have the same ingredients! How we use them is what we become.

One thing in your life that is renewed and keeps changing is your body.

There are those who see and those who listen. By opening your heart and mind you can do both.

Take time out and believe in yourself! Meditate and rejuvenate the mind, body and spirit.

There is no time, only space. For we have all the time in the world and then some.

There is no tomorrow, until today is finished.

When you give, you also receive.

Love is like a flower. You must plant the seed, nourish it, watch it grow, before you enjoy the beauty.

Bright days run into night, night stretches on forever through a blanket of stars. Beauty shines, lighting up the night, reflecting light in a three-dimensional world.

I wake up free of pain and strife on the wing of an Angel.

You have too little, you can't accept change, and you have no choices. In God's eyes you have all you have ask for.

God created all; Heaven, Earth, The Stars, but his greatest masterpiece was you.

Too Little to Late, to early? Make a choice!

Don't forget to breath; Now take a deep breath and exhale.

My door is open to you. Who is your door open to?

Never mind the clatter around you, listen to your heart.

Never forget the powerful being you are. You can do anything in life.

Rejoie with the Angels.

Your life is a Storybook.

If you never fall, how, will you know when you are standing.

Know both sides of life, the negative ad the positive. Then make the choice.

We all have choices.

Use your imagination to create something in your life.

How can you hear God's plan for you, if your line is always busy.?

Look at the miracles around you! A baby, butterfly, hummingbird, bumble bee.

You expect certain things from life, yet you accept less?

Angels surround you, talk to them!

Yes, there are earth Angles.

What do you value? Is it life?

Open your eyes and see what surrounds you.

What is on your Life Path?

Who does your thinking? You are man?

Everything stats with an idea.

Look within to find out who you are.

Many come, will you be chosen?

Today, try just being.

Make every moment count! For after this moment, it is forever gone.

Listen to the message of the Birds..

Spirit is the Supreme Creator! What are you?

Open the door and stand in the Light! Do you feel the warmth?

Your Palm is the Roadmap of your of your life. Your feet will carry

You along your path.

Think bigger, Think better! Be successful!

Carry inn your heart, better thoughts of tomorrow.

Embrace all that you are.

Look in the mirror and see someone you love.

Put your mind, body, and spirit, in the same place

at the same time.

Be the person you were meant to be.

Now, is the time to look within yourself.

Ying and Yang go together, Life's peanut butter

And jelly

If you never know the lows in life, how, will you

Ever know the highs?

Your thoughts are your own. Don't give them away.

If you were in Quicksand, what would it take to get you out?

Feel the Loving Spirit of Freedom.

A loving presence of Spirit surrounds you!

Seek wisdom from others.

Who is on your Path?

No amount of money is worth your conscious Freedom!

It is not a sin to Love! Love Yourself!

We eat, we drink, we rejoice in the love of God;

When we are in tune with Spirit, and the Angelic

realm.

Listen to the Whispers that come out of nowhere.

Listen to the Whispers in the Wind!

Chapter Twenty-Eight

THE NEW YEAR 2024

The New Year is upon us and everyone's going to start the New Year right, with resolutions! Of course, most won't keep them.

Let's look at the New Year. Lots of confusion, due to lots of wind, weather changes, tornado's will come through the country like wildfire, flattening many towns, some states will be hit twice as hard! Earthquakes will start really rocking the earth, from equator, to equator. The polarities are off and opening of the earth will take place. Stay away from Equator, San Salvador, and any place in between! Horrific hurricanes, the islands, Cancun will suffer again. Stay away from the shoreline of Mexico, the rebels are there and will create silly havoc on tourists.

Times are going to get harder, because people are living in fear! The energy is really starting to change! A part of California is going into the ocean; a tall mountain is going to crumble in Montana; somewhere in Yellowstone. Geysers are really going to be gushing upwards and outwards, beware of these things. Many will suffer and the Angelic realm says to take cover and duck! Go into hiding, if necessary, when the time comes near. Take precautions when you travel, especially around the Mississippi Valley, and areas of big rivers. Make sure all is well at home when you leave. The energy is going to do a lot of shifting and changing. Clearing the way for things to settle. Weather change will be cooler some places and hotter other places. All will end well. Hurricanes are going to erupt again, in volcanic ways. Spitting water in every direction, not caring where it lands, 200 mile an hour winds will prevail. Put on a life jacket, connect with your God self and stay safe in God's light. For once people listen, listen, listen, not to man but to your God self. Open your channel now and get tuned in to Spirit. You must learn to rely on yourself, not man, rely on yourself through God.

Our accomony is going to suffer, leaving us to depend on ourselves.

A beautiful summer will appear after lots of spring rains and storms. Summer will then be dry for most of the U.S.! Other parts of the world will flourish and bloom as gardens grow. It will take water to grow a garden in most of the US. Even Organ and Washington will be dry.

My resolution for the New Year is to come out alive, really alive and live with Spirit and the Angels guiding me higher to the next step. A Step above, always above! What a wonderful journey. What an exciting life. What a wonderful blessing, to truly experience life, free to live. Not exist or survive. But to truly know that living is not by accident, but through love.

I can tell you what is going to happen, I can help clear the past off your path, I can help prepare you, but you are the one who must live your life! To experience it, to turn a bad situation into something positive and good. To see the light in the darkness.

You are a more powerful being than you believe you are. Let the ego go and focus on the Spiritual side of you, your guides and Angels. Through you and your light many can see. Heal yourself and through you,others will heal.

The earth is a beautiful place to enjoy, live and experience life in human form. Look and you will see. Listen and you will learn. Speak and you will teach. We all have something to give; we all feel a need to learn. Make a New Years resolution to open yourself and live!

Quit dragging your past behind you, Leave the future ahead of you, and live for the moment! The Now!

Don't make plans, for plans sometime fail; don't criticize unless you, too, are above reproach. Be kinder to yourself and, in return, others will be kinder to you. A new you in a New Year; Enjoy!

Do not let the energy shifts or moons affect you! Be Positive! Send your positive energy out into a world of fear and darkness. Letting your light shine like the star you are. Surrounding yourself with love, joy and the Angelic realm! Healing and feeling the warmth of the sun's rays. There is nothing you cannot do for you are a powerful and wonderfully perfect person, made from Spirit.

Welcome to 2024 ! The New Beginning!

www.ingramcontent.com/pod-product-compliance
Lightning Source LLC
Chambersburg PA
CBHW051008140626
46546CB00016B/1343